Collecting Antiques

Collecting Antiques

Edited by
S. F. Ian Angus

Galahad Books
New York City

The editors would like to thank the following for the use of photographs for this book:
Ancient & Curious Ltd., Cyril Andrade Esq., Antique Porcelain Co., Ashmolean Museum, John Bell, of Aberdeen, Bethnal Green Museum, Biggs of Maidenhead, Birmingham Museum, J. W. Blanchard, Bracher & Sydenham, British Museum, Bruford & Son, Cameo Corner, Christies, Sterling Clerk Institute U.S.A., T. Copeland & Sons, Coxson Antiques, Cecil Davis, William Gordon Davis, Fitzwilliam Museum, Garrard & Co., Glaisher & Nash, John Hall, Hereford Corporation, Hotspur, Thomas Lumley, Malletts, Richard Mundey, Mrs. W. D. Munro, London Museum, Maxwell Joseph, Brian Nicholls of Oakham, Marjorie Parr, Redmont Philips, Pleasure of Things Past, Prides of London, G. S. Sanders, Science Museum, S. J. Shrubsole, Sothebys, Spink & Son, Temple Williams, Mrs. de Vere Green, Victoria & Albert Museum, Percy F. Wale Ltd., Josiah Wedgewood & Sons, W. H. Willson.

© Ward Lock Limited 1972
Published under arrangement with Ottenheimer Publishers, Inc.

Contents

Introduction

For all practical purposes the scope of English antiques is limited to the period from the Restoration of King Charles II in 1660 to the death of King George IV in 1830. In certain areas – furniture, for example, it is still possible for the collector of relatively modest means to go back farther in time and pick up Tudor chests or Jacobean chairs for a fraction of the sum demanded for a Chippendale bureau-bookcase. Pre-Restoration pewter is still obtainable, though prices have risen sharply in recent years. On the other hand, little English silver survived the depredations of the Civil War and the Commonwealth, while little had been achieved in the fields of glass and ceramics before the closing decades of the seventeenth century.

The eighteenth century, in which Britain lost one empire (America) and found another (India), inaugurated the Industrial Revolution, with its far-reaching consequences on the applied arts, and enjoyed an era of unparalleled prosperity; was the heyday of English silver, furniture, glass, pottery and porcelain and clocks. This was the age of such *maestros* as Paul de Lamerie, Chippendale, the Beilbys, Quare and Tompion. It witnessed the first brilliant flowering of English soft-paste porcelain and the wonderful decorative products of Chelsea, Derby, Bow and Worcester. It is a sad commentary, not only on the business methods of the period but on the response from the contemporary consumer, that Bow and Chelsea were soon forced into liquidation while Derby, Worcester and their successors had to lower their standards to remain commercially viable.

7

The lightness, elegance and restraint of eighteenth and early nineteenth century English antiques contrasts strangely with much of the products of the Victorian era. Nevertheless this is a period which cannot be overlooked. Apart from the gallant efforts of men like William Morris and Henry Cole, Christopher Dresser and Walter Crane, which redeemed the philistinism of the era in general, there are certain areas of Victoriana which, while characteristic of that age, have a strong appeal to the collector of the present day. Valentines and Christmas cards, posters and playbills and illustrated books – in the two-dimensional fields of graphics and typography the Victorians produced excellent material which is still available to the discerning collector for a modest outlay.

1. Furniture

Throughout its long history furniture has reflected, year by year, the changes in social conditions, the ebb and flow in this taste and that taste, the constantly changing habits of the people, the contrast between rich and poor, and the power of the community that made and used it to exercise authority over distant parts of the world and extract their riches. Silver, porcelain, jewellery and pewter are all dispensable; during periods of strife – such as the Civil War and the Commonwealth – they were hardly made at all. But even in war, men have a need, though limited, for basic items of furniture; and consequently furniture provides a continuous record of their needs and tastes.

In its design, furniture is closely related to architecture: the design of the inside of a house is a composition of furniture, carefully made and distributed, so that we find that all manner of architects turned their hands to furniture design. William Kent, Robert Adam and Charles Rennie Mackintosh are outstanding examples. Of course, this is to use the word 'furniture' in a very wide sense, but even if we were to exclude glass, porcelain, silver, chandeliers, fire-irons, carpets and paintings, it would still be true to say that the remaining articles – the tables and chairs and cabinets – are the most significant and imposing items in a room. They, together with the proportions of the room itself, and the shape of the windows, doors and fireplace, make up the design of the room, though they may be marred or enhanced by the lesser objects to the whole.

9

For the greater part of the Middle Ages there was very little furniture, either in the manor or in the cottage. What furniture that existed was generally portable, for the living space, even in the manor-house, was used for many purposes; it was only in monasteries and some of the greater castles that rooms were divided up according to their function. Tables were usually of the trestle type, made of oak, and had benches drawn up to them; only the most important members of society were allowed to sit in chairs. The most comfortable thing the ordinary person was likely to sit on was the settle, a bench with a high back and an arm at each end, and usually decorated with linen-fold panelling. The bed was the most valuable piece of furniture in any house, but even this could be dismantled and stored away. Lowly people, such as servants and students, had truckle beds, which were so low that they could be pushed away under a larger bed during the day. Things were stored in aumbrys, or in small chests which could also be used as side-tables. In general, medieval furniture was not of great quality, though there were magnificent linen-fold dressers and state beds. It was sturdily built, and the better pieces would be decorated with Gothic tracery in keeping with their surroundings, but not in any attempt to conceal their real purpose and shape, as in the neo-Gothic furniture of the nineteenth century.

In the sixteenth century furniture appeared that reflected the more settled lives that people lived under the Tudors. Houses now began to be divided up so that the whole family, not just the head of the house, could have some privacy. Bedrooms still remained fairly bare of furniture, but the parlours that began to appear at this time might have a number of pieces in them. The overall effect of the Tudor interior was rather dark, for the walls were covered with oak panelling and the furniture was mainly of dark oak, but some colour was added to the scene by tapestries or embroidered upholstery. The bed became an altogether more permanent and imposing piece of furniture, its four heavy posts bearing a carved wooden canopy or 'tester', over the top of the bed, which contained decorated panelling. The head-posts merged into the panelling at the head of the bed in the mid-sixteenth century and disappeared, while a feature of the remaining two posts and of the legs of tables in the late sixteenth century, was the decorative bulb, said to have been introduced to England by Huguenot refugees. These bulbs continued in use in the seventeenth century, and in fact reached their greatest size during the reign of James I, when they quite dominated the appearance of a piece of furniture. Another feature of the late-sixteenth century is the panel-back chair, which replaced the linen-fold chairs and the X-shape chairs of Henry VIII's day. The day-bed, a narrow bed with an adjustable headpiece for relaxing during the day, was probably brought to England by the foreign craftsmen whom Henry VIII introduced to work on his new palaces. In any case, they became a feature of the late Tudor household, for Shakespeare speaks at one point of 'lolling upon a lewd daybed'. Court cupboards, which appeared in the early sixteenth century, consisted of two tiers of open shelves, and were used to store cups, flagons, silver vessels and the like. Livery cupboards, through which air was allowed to circulate by means of balustered doors or open-work panels, were more suitable for food.

The quality of life continued to improve even more rapidly during the seventeenth century, and, after the restoration of Charles II, there began the period of elegance and magnificence that was to last until the social upheavals of the early nineteenth century. Furniture changed as the style of building changed from the Tudor mansions, with their large windows composed of long, thin lights, to the redbrick manor houses of the late-seventeenth century gentry and the Baroque extravagances of Bleinheim Palace. The rich discarded their heavy oak beds and replaced them with lighter, beechwood constructions, tall and slender and draped with hangings. At the four corners of the tester there appeared vase-shaped finials, covered with material and topped with ostrich plumes. The bed had ceased to be homely and become a fit subject for display. In the last third of the century marquetry became popular, and so, for the first time, did the taste for Chinese decoration. Both forms embellished late-seventeenth century cabinets, and they were succeeded by quieter arabesque patterns, using inlaid brass and tortoise-shell. The chest of drawers, which came into its own for the first time after the Restoration when extravagant dress was again acceptable, was similarly treated, at first with very colourful designs in marquetry of birds and flowers, and later, during William III's reign, with the overall 'seaweed' patterning of monochrome marquetry, drawn from the arabesque lines of the endive plant. Not that all forms of furniture followed the dictates of fashion, both in style and decoration, as interpreted in the Home Counties of England. The cupboard, for example, was a piece that continued to have a local life of its own, even in the eighteenth century. One example is the *cwpwedd tridarn* of Wales, predecessor of the farmhouse dresser.

Chairs became more sophisticated too. Panel-back chairs continued to be made until the 1660s, but after the Restoration there appeared chairs with twisted legs and backs formed of turned balusters. There was a new accent on comfort, too, with the appearance of the upholstered, winged armchair. The settee was another late-seventeenth century development, derived partly from the settle, partly from an expansion of the chair. In its early days it looked rather like two or more chairs joined together, for its length was divided up by arms and its back was formed of a series of chair backs, either open or upholstered.

The long dining-table became obsolete in the late seventeenth century, for it was now more acceptable to dine even a large company in groups round small, scattered tables. For such occasions the gateleg table was more suitable. This usually rather plain table was normally round or oval when its flaps were extended. The side-table was a better subject for decoration, for the examples delicately carved by the hand of Grinling Gibbons, master of the art of carving flowers, fruit and birds in a startlingly realistic manner, are by no means normal among the side-tables of the later seventeenth century. The Restoration side-table was frequently in walnut and had twisted or baluster legs; while the French influence followed in the train of William III, so that side-tables displayed tapered legs with gadrooned capitals, foliated strapwork pendants and elaborately scrolled stretchers.

The development of seventeenth century furniture was rather haphazard in comparison with that of the eighteenth century. All kinds of influences were at work, both from home and abroad, and furniture makers were affected by the decorative ideas of such men as Grinling Gibbons and Daniel Marot. But in the eighteenth and early nineteenth centuries, though design continued to be affected by ideas from all kinds of quarters – the taste for *chinoiserie* and the Gothic style are examples – the work of the designers was far more important. They introduced some consistency into furniture design. By no means was every piece of work made from their designs, yet almost every piece was affected by the publication of such books of design as Chippendale's *Gentleman and Cabinet-Maker's Director*, which made them known to everyone in the furniture trade.

The outstanding designers of this period were William Kent, Thomas Chippendale, Robert Adam, George Hepplewhite and Thomas Sheraton. Kent (1684–1748) was by no means exclusively a furniture designer. He began as a painter and later became an architect and sculptor, even helping to establish the style of the eighteenth century English landscape garden. His studies in Italy made him an enthusiastic follower of Palladio, and when he began to design furniture in England he developed the architectural motifs to which he had become so attached. As a result his furniture was on the grand scale.

The London cabinet-maker Thomas Chippendale (1718–1779) had a much wider-ranging talent as a furniture designer, for he assimilated the new fashions as they appeared and produced his own finely designed versions of the Rococo style, the Chinese Taste and the Gothic Taste, and, late in his career, the Neoclassical style. His beds were lighter in appearance than those of his predecessors, with carved mahogany posts, cabriole legs on lion's feet and delicately carved shafts. His bookcases too, though they included architectural motifs such as the broken pediment, were altogether lighter than Kent's pieces. Many remember him best for the design of his chairs, like the ribbon-back and the classical chairs with oval-, heart- or shield-shaped backs, and the tapered classical leg in place of the cabriole leg.

What Robert Adam (1728–1792) sought to do in furniture differs not at all from his work as an architect, for he conceived architecture and furniture as merely different facets of the same problem of design. Adam admired 'the rise and fall, the advance and recess, and other diversity of forms' in a building, as well as 'a variety of light mouldings', and it was the same principles that he applied in his interiors, such as that magnificent example, the library at Syon House. Here the pastel shade walls are decorated with classical style mouldings in white, and the circular portraits in oils do not exist in their own right but all form part of the overall design.

George Hepplewhite, who died in 1786, was another London furniture maker whose designs were published after his death as *The Cabinet-maker and Upholsterer's Guide*. The Neo-classical style was a strong influence in his work. There are Hepplewhite style bookcases, for example, with straight moulded cornices, surmounted by an urn or some scrollwork, and the doors banded with satinwood and sometimes enriched with an inlay of figures. His beds had slender posts carved with wheatears, and cornices inlaid or painted with flowers or ribbons; and his chairs had the classical motifs of shield- or heart-shaped backs.

Thomas Sheraton (1750–1806) straddles both the late-eighteenth century period and the Regency. He published a number of books of design, notably the *Cabinet-maker and Upholsterer's Drawing Book* and the *Cabinet-maker's Dictionary*. His early style had a great deal in common with the work of Hepplewhite, but his bookcases, for example, tended to be narrower with rather stilted proportions, and to include features such as swan-necks and serpentine pediments, unusual finials, and satinwood veneers. He used the classical urn as a feature in some of his chairs in the 1790s as well as making square-back chairs.

The Regency style was pioneered by the architect Sir John Soane, and Thomas Hope, a writer and amateur furniture designer. The style was based, in part at least, on a close study of Roman interior decoration, though the Egyptian sphinx was also imported. The whole effect must have been extremely severe. There were sofas that followed the supposed design of Roman couches, with a low back curved over at one end, and the tripod table that the Romans had made in marble was reproduced in wood. Lion masks and swans were frequent features of the style, as was the hocked animal leg support, topped by a cat or lion head. Many of the decorative features were made of brass, so that there was no need for the furniture makers to have any skill in carving. Alternatively, items such as chairs might be made of beechwood painted black and decorated with a design in gold.

It was obvious that a profound change was bound to come over furniture as the nineteenth century progressed. England had a growing middle class, all of whom wanted to dress up their houses as they thought was befitting to their station, and so the manufacturers, flooded with orders, sought to do the job more rapidly and brought in mechanized processes.

The Victorians used machinery to make their furniture, but they tried at the same time to make the same kind of furniture their forefathers had made – with certain improvements. Two things were required of a piece of furniture: that it should be comfortable, if it was going to be sat on, and that it should be imposing. The result: massive armchairs, that look even heavier than they really are, profusely decorated with carving, and every piece of the structure curving and bulging this way and that; or massive pieces of 'Gothic' furniture, whether they be like Pugin's cabinets, covered all over with Gothic designs, or the plainer, sturdy and austere beds, washbasins and cabinets designed by William Burges. The first sign of change came in the 1870s with Morris and the Arts and Crafts Movement. Part of this was backward-looking with its accent on hand-produced furniture of a medieval simplicity. Men with real talent as designers – such as A. H. Macmurdo, C. R. Mackintosh and Charles Voysey – began to work on furniture once again. They totally rejected the clutter of the Victorian sitting room in which every surface was decorated and every flat space filled with a knick-knack of some kind. What really astonishes one about the interior designs of Mackintosh, for example, is their remarkable simplicity; a room is designed as a whole (just as Kent and Adam did) and the maximum use is made of the space available.

A late-sixteenth century chair has its
original cresting and turned finials.
About 1580.

A late Elizabethan stool of unusual
shape. The frieze is shaped and
carved on the lower edges.
About 1580.

Opposite

Above A George I side-table made of pine and panel gilt with a marble top.
A lion's mask in the centre of the frieze. About 1720.

Below A pair of Sheraton painted tub chairs, upholstered in green silk.
About 1790.

16

Above An eighteenth century walnut marquetry side-table with Bombé-form front and sides. About 1740.

Right A George II mahogany chair with stuffed back and covered with mid-eighteenth century Soho tapestry.

18

A very small gateleg table in figured oak. It has eight baluster legs with knurled feet. It measures 2 feet 7 inches across the top. About 1680.

19

A Sheraton bow-fronted chest of drawers, made in faded mahogany with original handles.

A beautiful mahogany tall-boy of about 1760 with perfectly matched graining.

A claw and ball tripod table in mahogany with a revolving top. Chippendale style about 1760.

A Sheraton mahogany sideboard.

Opposite
Above   A Sheraton mahogany banquet table with two hinged leaves and semi-circular ends. About 1790.

Below   A Sheraton George III card table in rosewood with a folding top inlaid with satinwood and rosewood.

23

A Chippendale mahogany wing chair.

A George III mahogany chair in the Hepplewhite style. The seat is striped horsehair.

Opposite

Above　A Hepplewhite mahogany break-fronted bookcase. About 1790.

Below　A George III carved mahogany love-seat of serpentine design. It is covered in red leather.

25

Above   A Sheraton tambour desk in satinwood. About 1790.

Above Right   A mahogany chiffonier with brass gallery and trellis-doors backed with silk. About 1810.

Right   A Wellington Chest in mahogany. About 1833.

26

Top Left   A mahogany davenport with the writing slide lined with green leather. About 1820.

Top Right   A Regency mahogany worktable supported on an X-frame and stand.

Above   A dining-table carved in oak with a statue of St. George slaying the dragon on the central stretcher. Probably designed by A. W. Pugin, it was made by George Myers about 1850.

27

2. Silver

The Restoration of Charles II in 1660 is usually thought to mark the beginning of the period of domestic silver. The Church during the Middle Ages had been the patron of the arts, but the ravages of the Reformation had taken a heavy toll of its medieval treasures. Added to that there had been the heavy demands of war over the centuries, the lavish gifts made to foreign potentates, and, finally, the wholesale destruction of plate to support one side or the other during the Civil War – quite apart from wear and tear and the common habit of melting down plate, to have it refashioned. For the collector, especially the beginner; pre-Restoration silver, even small articles such as spoons, beakers, tumbler cups and wine tasters, is often beyond reach. This is not to suggest that silver of the medieval, Tudor and early Stuart periods should be ignored.

The Restoration coincided with new developments in science and industry, art and architecture, trade and overseas trade and commerce. Those who had joined the royal family in exile returned and set about rebuilding their lives and estates. There were the large and prosperous middle classes, all quite prepared to emulate their wealthier neighbours. For the silversmith, the return of Charles II in May, 1660, was the beginning of a long era of work and prosperity. With trade at its lowest ebb there were problems, but the craft promptly celebrated the occasion by deciding to change the annual date-letter (struck on all plate) from the traditional May 19th, St. Dunstan's Day, to May 29th, the King's birthday. At this time there was an upsurge of demand for bold and showy silver and silvergilt. As usual, the impetus came from abroad, and now the returning court brought new styles home with them. Both France and Holland wielded great influence on silver design.

The two-handled cups, variously called porringers, caudle cups and posset cups, are probably the most typical of all Charles II silverwares. Posset and caudle were both spiced milk drinks, curdled with wine or ale and taken hot, so that handled cups were very necessary. The rather squat bulging bodies of these cups were usually embossed and chased with flowers, foliage and animals. A typical feature of the bulging-bodied porringers was the cast caryatid handles, which became progressively more spindly and more formalized, so that some appear as slender, double scrolls with leafy blobs for heads.

By this time the days of the high table were virtually over, so that silver for show was more likely to be in the form of garnitures for the mantelpiece or fireplace – vases and jars with no other purpose but to gleam and look splendid in firelight and candlelight. Between ten and fifteen inches high, they are typically enriched with floral and foliate embossing enclosing cherubs or masks and with richly festooned applied work round the necks.

Equally richly ornamented were the silver sconces for one or two candles, with shaped oval back-plates, and the impressive toilet services with perhaps a dozen or sixteen pieces, including mirror, jewel caskets, pin cushion, flasks, flagons and dishes and even covered bowls elaborately chased with scrolls, leafage and *amorini* in high relief.

Cut-card ornament was introduced from France about this time and consisted of thin silhouettes of silver soldered round the bases of bowls and cups, and round finials and handle sockets, being an effective way of helping to strengthen thin-gauge metal. Some silver, notably tankards, wine cups and the heavy-based small tumbler cups, on the whole escaped the current passion for overall decoration, other than perhaps a band of acanthus leaf chasing or an engraved coat-of-arms in a plumed mantling.

In the Commonwealth period, the beer tankard had a spreading base, aptly called a skirt foot, and replaced the so-called 'Puritan' type with its base in one with the body and without a foot. By 1660, the rim foot and a slightly tapering cylindrical barrel was the basic form of tankard and was to be little changed for more than half a century. Unlike the handles on bowls and cups, tankard handles were broad scrolls, sometimes with hoof-like terminals, and with a cast, bifurcated or two-lobed thumbpiece. Tankards were almost always covered, the lid being a flat-domed cap with a small wavy or pointed peak at the front. Base and lip were usually simply moulded or reeded.

Wine cups had a trumpet-shaped bowl and simple baluster stem on a circular moulded foot. Following a really old-established tradition were the small beakers, made in various sizes from about two and a half to seven inches high. They had cylindrical bodies flaring to the rims, and might be plain or decorative as taste and money dictated. Another commonplace in silver were the delightful little tumbler cups which were probably used for spirits or other strong liquors. Rarely more than a couple of inches high, they are heavy-based so that they return to upright even if tilted.

The Baroque style, which came in about 1670 was really a formalizing of the Dutch naturalistic style. The emphasis was still on embossing and chasing, but they became more restrained. Alternating palm and acanthus leaf chasing was arranged around the bases of cups and tankards or round the broad rims of dishes. Fluting, both straight and swirled, was similarly used on the lower parts of drinking vessels, and it was a style admirably suited to the column candlesticks of the period, which gradually became plainer until ousted by the cast baluster candlestick in the 1680s.

Chinoiserie, or decoration in the Chinese taste, has been a recurrent style in the history of English silver. Its earliest manifestation, from about 1675 to 1690, appears to have been one of the few entirely English decorative inventions. Lightly sketched and rather inaccurate palm trees, spiky foliage, and flowers provided a setting for warriors in short tunics or sages in flowing kimonos, for temples and pavilions and for exotic birds and butterflies.

Tea, coffee and chocolate, all of which were introduced to England about the middle of the century, quickly became fashionable and needed silverware from which they could be served. The silversmiths' reaction was to adapt the tall flagon, making a tall, tapering, cylindrical pot with a spout and handle. The only difference between the pots for the two drinks being the provision of a small hinged lid within the cover to the chocolate-pot through which the stirrer rod could be inserted. Most of the earliest surviving teapots resemble small Chinese winepots, perhaps derived from porcelain or stoneware originals.

The second half of the seventeenth century saw a large rise in the consumption of both sugar and spices, and the first casters in silver date from the reign of Charles II. Here again, the straight-sided cylinder provided the basic style, with a high domed, pierced cover held in place by sturdy bayonet clamps. Casters called for little decoration, and ornament was chiefly restricted to piercing, a shallow band of fluting or acanthus chasing, cut-card work or engraving.

Many persecuted Huguenots fled to England after the Edict of Nantes in 1685, among them the brilliant craftsman, Pierre Harache. They brought with them, no doubt, the design books they used in their native towns of Metz, Rouen, Poitou and so on – design books that laid emphasis on the detailed ornament known in France as *Régence* – ordered arrangements of strapwork enclosing scrolls, shells, husks and foliage, of applied lion and human head masks, of delicate cut-card and other applied work. They also brought a new variety of forms, based chiefly on the baluster shape. They introduced the cast baluster candlestick and ousted the fluted column type; they turned the straight-sided flagon into a graceful ewer with a broad high lip and flying-scroll handle; they heightened the two-handled cup, making it well-proportioned and elegant with a moulded rib round the body together with sturdy scroll- or harp-shaped handles, thus ridding the silversmiths' shelves for good and all of bulging-bodied cups and coarse and ungainly embossing.

From the time of the great influx of Huguenot craftsmen two distinct styles emerged – one continuing the traditions of English baroque, the other of definitely French inspiration. At times, the two merged. Silver for coffee, for instance, largely remained in the English tradition. Established, too, was the baluster cast candlestick (though the earliest ones were in fact the work of Pierre Harache in the early 1680s); with moulded, octagonal bases with sunk centres and knopped stems with cylindrical sockets, they set the style for the next half-century.

31

So great was the demand for silverwares that not a few silver-smiths were apparently using the coinage of the realm to make plate. In March, 1697, the Act 'for encouraging the bringing in of wrought plate to be coined' reversed the process. In addition, all new wrought silver had to be of a higher standard of fineness than sterling, which had been in force since 1300. This higher standard silver, containing 3·3 per cent more silver, was known as the *Britannia Standard* because the plate had to be marked by the assay offices with a punch showing 'the figure of a woman commonly called Britannia'. The period of Britannia silver lasted from March, 1697, until June, 1720. Silver of this period was frequently quite plain, relying for its appeal on the beauty of line and the soft reflected mouldings.

In the early years of the Britannia period, coinciding with the reign of Queen Anne, the Huguenot styles gradually gained an ascendancy over the native ones. The baluster form soon domin-ated most silverwares. Coasters, candlesticks, jugs and teapots showed gracious curves. Coffee pots, though mostly straight-sided, conformed with curving swan-necked spouts and scroll handles. Even some mugs and tankards appeared with a tucked-in base on a circular moulded foot. The teapot of the Queen Anne period had grown away from the winepot style into a squat pear shape, with a high-domed cover and curved spout. Following suit was an addition to the tea-table – the tea-kettle, provided with a baluster-legged stand and a spirit lamp or charcoal brazier beneath. Only the tea-caddy stayed firmly unaffected by the baluster curve, remaining an oblong or octagonal canister, usually with a bottle-like top and sliding base.

Entirely French in conception, and almost always made by French silversmiths in England, were helmet-shaped jugs and ewers. They were generally mounted on a circular, moulded foot, and the body was divided by two ribs. The upper one followed the outline of the rim and spout and usually featured an applied mask or other decoration immediately below the spout. The flying-scroll handle was sometimes cast as an arching caryatid while the bases were usually, though not invariably, enriched with applied work.

Applied detail and engraving were the two great decorative treatments of the Queen Anne period. Though much domestic

32

silver was relatively plain, few important 'state' pieces were left unadorned. At the turn of the century there was a revival and a refinement of cut-card ornament.

Engraving on silver was of an exceptionally high order during the reigns of William III, Queen Anne and George I, and a number of very beautiful salvers and dishes have survived. In contrast, some salvers and waiters were plain, or decorated no more than with a moulded or gadrooned rim and an engraved coat-of-arms or crest. Variety was sometimes achieved by the form only – square, circular, octagonal, hexagonal or multi-lobed. Shallow dishes with fluted edges, known as strawberry dishes, were made in various sizes from small saucer types to large bowls, some nine or ten inches in diameter. These too, might be left plain, or delicately chased or engraved within each of the flutes.

The reign of George I saw the new age of the dining service. Plates and dishes in silver were nothing new, but now there were also soup tureens, sauce boats, and knives, forks and spoons made *en suite*. Forks in England had been rather late arrivals (those made prior to 1690 being very rare indeed). They were, however, included among the dinner-table wares of the early eighteenth century home. About the turn of the seventeenth century, the trifid end of spoons and forks became rounded-off to the shield top, with a flattened stem and a rat-tail down the back of the spoon-bowl. Forks were sometimes two-pronged, usually three-pronged. During the reign of Queen Anne, the shield top was replaced by the round end, known as Hanoverian, but still with a plain rat-tail. Hanoverian remained the favourite pattern of flatware until superseded by Old English in the later eighteenth century, and by more decorative patterns during the Regency.

About 1750 there was another revival of chinoiserie, this time executed in repoussé designs and in pierced work. It was an aptly popular fashion for all kinds of tea-table silver. As often as not, the chinoiserie designs were inextricably mixed with the scrolls and shells of the rococo style.

During the 1760s pagoda-like roofs, Chinese figures and temple bells appeared on the elaborately pierced basket epergnes used as table centrepieces on formal occasions. The bridges, coolie figures, palm trees and strange plants associated by the English silversmiths with Chinese art were used with considerable delicacy for the pierced baskets and epergne stands. Even pierced salts with cut-glass bowls were made in that style about 1760.

By the middle 1760s, even the most eager rococo-ists were tiring of this style. Some silversmiths tended to look again across the Channel and to formalize silver in the French manner once more. Tureens were made shallower, with wavy rims and finials in the form of fruit or vegetables, rather like those made in porcelain. Sometimes ripple-fluted effects were achieved. The excavations of classical sites at Palmyra, Baalbek, Rome and Herculaneum were of great interest at this time and artists and architects visited the sites. Among them was the young Scottish architect, Robert Adam. The acknowledged aim of the neo-classicists was to draw on 'the most elegant ornament of the most refined Grecian articles'. Laurel wreaths and festoons, anthemion, palmette and scroll borders were neat and restrained after the contorted cult of rococoism. The stone urn and the vase provided an elegant new shape for silver.

A development of engraving called bright-cut was particularly suited to the Adam designs that soon came to be made in silver. Fluting was equally suitable for echoing the slender marble pillars and pilasters beloved of Adam, and it was also well suited to the new stamping processes which were being used, especially in Sheffield, for making candlesticks.

The very simplicity of the vase and the oval made them suitable for teapots, tea urns, sugar bowls and swing-handled baskets, soup and sauce tureens as well as for the ubiquitous cups and covers. The classical column was tapered, and topped with an urn finial for candlesticks and candelabra. Beading and reeding were the most favoured border ornaments. Interest was added to pierced boat-shapes by using deep-blue glass liners.

The success of Adam and the neo-classicists lay in their elegant, delicate designs, but Wyatt and Henry Holland had more grandiose tendencies, while by 1800 even the King voiced an opinion that 'the Adams have introduced too much of neatness and prettiness'. In silver, however, the 'sippets of embroidery' had already started to give way to a grander style by the 1790s. There was more pronounced and even applied decoration overlaying the simplicity of the Grecian. Festoons, once only bright-cut, were now chased with a Roman majesty; small applied medallions,

34

modelled of course on classical lines, were used particularly by Fogelburg and Gilvert on jugs and teapots. Lion masks once again appeared at the knuckles of sauce boats and footed tureens; bold leafage, ovolos and scrolls in relief, and reed-and-tie borders began to supersede beading and simple reeding.

After 1790 all sign of Adam's grace vanished. 'Massiveness', boomed C. H. Tatham, 'is the principal characteristic of good Plate,' and 'good Chasing . . . a branch of Sculpture.' At Rundell & Bridge's behest men such as Tatham, John Flaxman and Stothard turned the silversmith into a vehicle for producing sculpture in silver.

The craft of the silversmith, like so many other crafts, could not escape the onslaught of the Industrial Revolution with its machines and mass-production techniques. In Birmingham and Sheffield in particular stamping presses were turning out copies of fashionable silver., For quite a long time, the machine-made products were reasonably well designed. Sheffield candlesticks were, indeed, good examples of silver made by stamping in sections, assembly and loading. The London silversmiths were still, on the whole, hand craftsmen, but they, too, were caught in the net of Victorian grandiosity for its own sake.

Sheffield Plate was introduced as a substitute for silver and to provide a wider public with pleasant and decorative wares. In 1840 the invention of electroplating meant yet another new technique with which silver had to compete. The early Victorian period, with its huge industrial upheavals, its quickly rich and its multiplying poor, changed the face of Britain. The Victorians did not, however, stifle craftsmanship. They extolled it. Even so, the relentless progress of industrialization and mass production ended the great period of English craft silver.

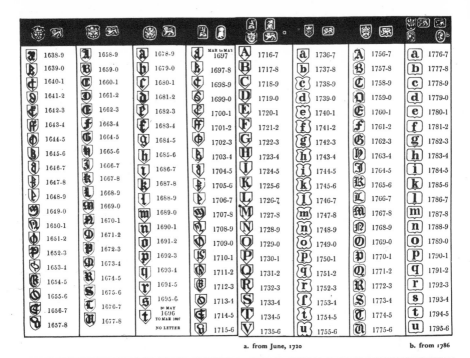

MAR to MAY 1697

a. from June, 1720

b. from 1786

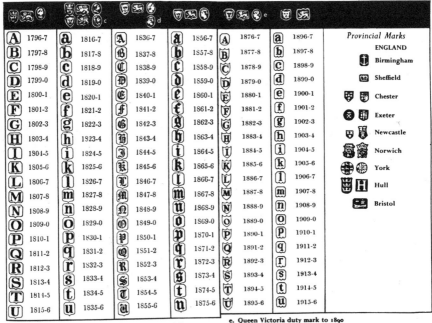

c. from 1821

d. from 1837

e. Queen Victoria duty mark to 1890

Provincial Marks

ENGLAND

Birmingham

Sheffield

Chester

Exeter

Newcastle

Norwich

York

Hull

Bristol

Above is the complete list of assay-office marks from 1638–1916.

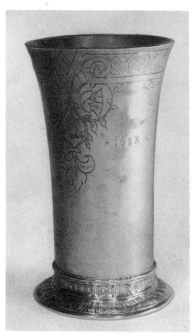

Left The traditional beaker which preceded glass as the universal drinking vessel. It was made by a smith using the mark G.C., for the Mitchell family of Somerset.

Below A pair of Charles II candlesticks. They were made in 1666 by a smith using a crowned S.

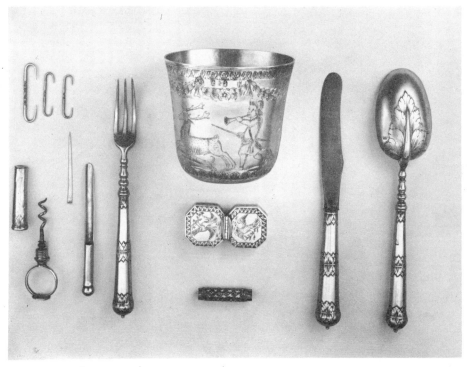

A ginger jar made about 1675 has the maker's mark of IB with a crescent below.

This coffee pot by Anthony Nelme in 1701 shows the typical design of this period.

Opposite

Above Right A plain-body tankard of the Charles II type. It was made in 1661 by a smith who used an 'Orb and cross'. Note position of hall marks.

Above Left A porringer of 1691 is engraved with chinoiseries and has slender scroll handles.

Below This travelling set, which folds up into the cup, includes a double-spice box, nutmeg grater, apple-corer and toothpick. The cup was made by Charles Overing in 1701.

A simple bullet-shaped teapot with engraved coat-of-arms and foliate
decoration. Made by Gabriel Sleath in 1733.

Opposite

Above Left   A pair of baluster candlesticks dated 1725 by Thomas Mason.

Above Right   A highly rococo two-handled cup and cover made by Paul de
Lamerie in 1733.

Below   A set of three Queen Anne casters made by David Willaume.

A tea-kettle with its own stand and spirit-lamp, which was made by Edward Vincent in 1734.

A small coffee pot by Charles Kandler.

Opposite

Above An inkstand on four scroll feet and made by William Cripps in 1747.

Below Two sauce boats made by Daniel Piers in 1749. Note the unusual 'quilted' decoration on the feet and double-scroll handles.

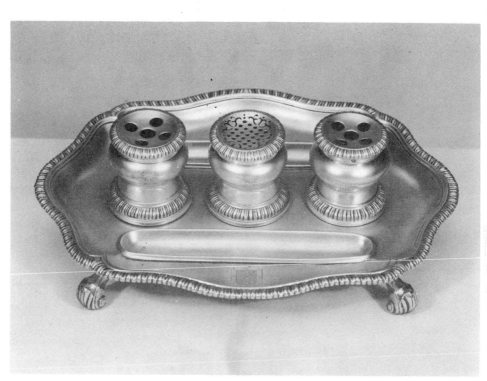

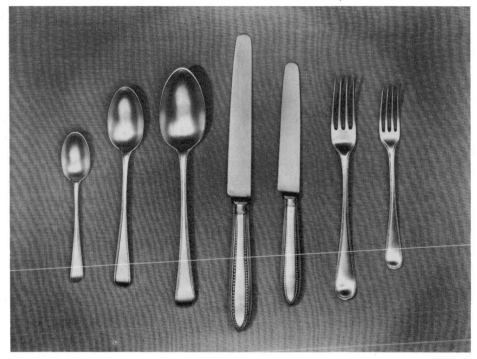

A set of beaded-border cutlery dating from between 1775 and 1781. It is rare to find a complete set.

Opposite

Above   A teapot made in 1790 by Peter and Jonathon Bateman, of the famous Bateman family.

Below   A large tray (23 inches wide) made by John Crouch and Thomas Hannam in 1793.

A five-piece tea-table service made in the popular melon shape by William Eaton in 1822–23. Note the unusually large sugar bowl and cream jug.

3. Pottery and Porcelain

At some time in the distant past and in different countries, the early kiln-baked clays, called earthenwares, were improved upon – by design or more probably accident – in different ways. Thus, an earthenware made of some kind of natural clay was subjected to a much higher kiln temperature to become stoneware – a much harder vitrified material which was impervious to water – while the addition of other substances, notably china-clay (kaolin) and china-stone (petuntse) was found to give the translucency which is the main characteristic of porcelain. Certain non-porosity and added beauty was given by a protecting layer of glaze (or glass), which was probably an early Egyptian invention. It is found with few exceptions upon earthenware, stoneware and porcelain. When the Romans occupied Britain they made much fine pottery, but on their departure the craft was continued only by itinerant potters who worked wherever they found suitable clay until local needs had been supplied. This kind of medieval pottery was usually clumsy, often misshapen, and covered with a green, brown or yellow lead glaze. Decoration was mainly incised (or scratched), impressed or applied in the form of shaped pads of clay. The potter used for this purpose anything that came to hand, bits of twig, sea-shells, and so on. There were no decorators, as we understand the term, in those days.

During the fifteenth century potteries were established at many centres, among them London, Wrotham in Kent, Staffordshire, Derbyshire and Cheshire. Decoration in colour was introduced, notably in the form of applied decoration in contrasting colours which led to the popularity of what are known as *slip wares* in the seventeenth century. This kind of pottery, which is associated particularly with a family of Staffordshire potters by the name of Toft, is today rare and much sought after. It has no refinement and was never intended to be other than functional. The simple process of manufacture was that upon a red clay body a mixture of white clay and water (*slip* as it is called) was worked into patterns of wavy and dotted lines, flowers and leaves, animals and birds, and crude human figures and busts, before the whole was covered with lead glaze. Some pieces bear names which may be either those of the makers or of intended recipients.

Towards the end of the seventeenth century a handful of potters began to experiment with stoneware, in imitation of the ware then being made by a Meissen (Dresden) potter named Johan Böttger, who in turn had already copied from the Chinese. The best known of the English potters are John Dwight of Fulham, who perfected a lovely white stoneware, and John and David Elers, whose red and black ware was lathe-turned in formal geometrical patterns or else bore applied ornament which had been stamped out in metal dies. This '*sprigged*' decoration was developed by John Astbury, an early eighteenth century potter who worked very much in the Elers style, though his ware was glazed whereas Astbury's was not.

Though no glaze was really needed on stoneware, another class of seventeenth century ware is known by the name of '*salt-glazed*', because it was glazed with salt thrown into the kiln at a temperature of over 2,000°F; this resulted in the characteristic, slightly pitted, orange-skin appearance. The white surface of the early ware was sometimes decorated with incised design which was then filled in with blue pigment. Stoneware was further developed right into the eighteenth century, culminating in a spate of colourful, jewel-like enamelling in the Chinese and continental styles, but at the same time lead-glazed pottery was greatly improved. Whieldon made figures and also perfected the use of mingled glazes in different colours in what are known as his 'tortoiseshell' wares. While working for Wedgwood he used a fine green glaze on moulded articles such as the well known 'cauliflower' teapots and tea-caddies. During the eighteenth century, too, Ralph Wood of Burslem followed the Astbury tradition in the making of mantelpiece figures and the still very popular Toby jug to be followed by his descendants and many others who developed the Staffordshire figures which are so sought after today.

Early in the eighteenth century attempts were made at imitating Chinese porcelain; this resulted in the making of what is known as 'delft' in Holland and Britain, 'maiolica' in Italy and Spain and 'faience' in Germany and France. The only similarity between porcelain and delft lay in the white surface colour and in the Chinese style decoration which was applied to it. Whereas true porcelain is translucent, delft is not, being merely ordinary earthenware covered with a white tin-oxide based glaze, the powdery texture of which demanded bold, clean brushwork. We speak of the 'delft painter's touch' when we consider this kind of necessarily coarse decoration, which is found upon the delft made between 1600 and 1770 at London, Bristol and Liverpool.

Certain continental potters experimented successfully with translucent porcelain as early as 1580, but not until 1710 was anything done on a large scale; it was at Meissen that Böttger found out that the true porcelain of the Far East was composed of a mixture of china-clay and china-stone. Then, in 1745, the chemists at Vincennes evolved their own kind of porcelain, an imitation made of china-clay and a fritt of powdered glass which we now call 'soft paste' or 'artificial' porcelain. It was this kind of substitute which English potters successfully developed. At Bow, Thomas Frye and Edward Heylyn took out a patent in 1744 and a factory was established at Chelsea perhaps even a little earlier. These were followed soon after 1750 by rival concerns at Bristol, Worcester, Derby, Lowestoft, Liverpool and Longton Hall in Staffordshire – all making soft paste porcelains of varying compositions. Then in 1768, William Cockworthy found out how to make true porcelain, probably quite by accident, and set up a factory in Plymouth which was later moved to Bristol and finally to New Hall in the Potteries.

Every now and then innovators tried with varying degrees of success to market new and improved *pastes* (bodies). Thus, in the 1820s, William Billingsley, chemist and china-painter, invented a most attractive paste which he made at Pinxton, Nantgarw and Swansea until ruinous kiln losses brought failure and a return to the old position of paid decorator in another's factory. The established factories introduced paste after paste, always striving after perfection, until with all the resources of the great potting centre of Staffordshire behind them, Spodes perfected and introduced, soon after 1800, a new body in which china-clay and china-stone were reinforced with calcined bone or *bone-ash*. It was not long before variations of this new paste had replaced every other kind, and there has been little change in its composition since.

When English potters first made porcelain they had no previous experience in the decorating of it, for the old styles, which suited earthenware were not sympathetic to the more delicate ware. It is true that now and again, on Liverpool wares in particular, we recognize the bold brushwork of a delft painter, but by and large the decoration on early English porcelain was the result of a new technique, and the popular styles were copied from foreign sources. At first, because Chinese porcelain was so popular and familiar, decoration was carried out in the Chinese style, in blue or in enamels. Occasionally the exotic Oriental designs were copied exactly, but more usually the separate motifs, the mandarin figures, the flowering shrubs, the dragons, the pagodas and so on were used in endless combinations to form the kind of patterns which Europeans expected to see. The over-worked *Willow Pattern*, though of later date, is a typical example of the kind of decoration which no Chinese artist could possibly ever perpetrate. Very few Japanese patterns were copied, apart from those in the style of a seventeenth century potter named Kakiemon, which may be seen on Worcester and Bow porcelains as 'wheat-sheaf', 'banded hedge', 'quail' and 'partridge'.

From the famous Meissen factory, on the outskirts of Dresden, much fine porcelain was exported to England, and its designs (many of which were adaptations of Chinese originals) were copied by English decorators between about 1760 and 1770 while at the same time the Oriental taste gradually fell into disfavour. The German styles which quickly became popular included landscapes, harbour scenes and naturalistic birds; but the greatest influence on British porcelain decoration came from the lovely flowers and the wonderfully colourful, entirely imaginary creatures known as 'exotic birds', which at Worcester, rendered in different styles by innumerable artists, were set on scale-blue grounds to splendidly brilliant effect. The flower painting took three distinct forms; formal Oriental flowers (*Indianische Blumen*), naturalistic flowers (*Streu Blumen*), and bouquets and sprigs of idealized flowers (*Meissner Blumen*).

During the time of this predominance of the German styles it was inevitable that the influence of the second great continental factory at Sèvres in France, should have some effect on English design, and when the Meissen factory was taken over by the Prussians in 1763 the resultant disorganization gave the French their chance to oust their rivals as dictators of fashion in porcelain decoration. The effect, between 1770 and the end of the century, is seen on English wares in the shape of a spate of wonderful ground (all-over) colours such as *bleu-de-roi*, *bleu celeste* (turquoise), apple, pea and sea-greens, and *Rose Pompadour* (claret), often allied to magnificent gilded patterning of every kind. We see, too, on Chelsea, Derby and Worcester wares in particular, a great variety of delicate arrangements of floral and foliage festoons, seen to typical effect in the Worcester 'hop trellis' patterns.

Porcelain decoration after 1800 – the Victorian Age – is too vast and complex a subject to be adequately described in these pages. The significant point is that with technical and production difficulties more or less overcome there was no limit to possible extravagance in decoration, and an extravagance which was in fact welcomed by a new kind of public who could afford the best and who wanted its value to be obvious. The porcelain body was used more and more as merely a surface to receive fine painting in every conceivable style, and though sometimes the older, still-flourishing factories such as Derby and Worcester carried on their old traditions of restrained design, even in their wares technical perfection may sometimes seem a poor exchange for the inexplicable but real attraction of their imperfect early productions – at least in the eyes of the collector. At the beginning of course, few factories had their own staff of proficient, trained decorators, and special or difficult work was often entrusted to 'outside decorators' in London or elsewhere. On the other hand every nineteenth century factory of any importance had its own properly trained artists, many of them specialists, and many of them known to us by their styles and sometimes by their names. The result is that the collector of later wares must perforce be interested more in decoration than in the paste upon which it rests, particularly since this was more or less standardized throughout the industry.

A Lambert Delft posset pot painted in blue, red and green with crude imitations of Chinese moths. About 1700.

A lead-glazed earthenware jug
inscribed on the front –

    R
– 'EE 1671' – in slack slip.

A Staffordshire mantelpiece ornament in the shape of a Dove-cote, it stands on paw feet and the drawer pulls open. It is painted with enamels. About 1780.

Right　A Bow inkwell in porcelain, painted in 'famille verte' enamels and dated 1750.

Below　A Bow figure of the actress Kitty Clive in her role as the 'Fine Lady' in Garrick's farce 'Lethe'. The date 1750 is incised inside the base. .

Opposite

Above Left　A salt-glazed monogrammed plate painted in Grilliat enamels. About 1760.

Above Right　A kneeling Chinaman painted in enamels and marked 'SPODE' in red. About 1800.

Below　A pair of vases and matching ewer decorated in the Chinese style by Mason. About 1835.

54

Top A Chelsea carp tureen of the red anchor period and stand to match. About 1755.

Above A pair of Longton Hall leaf-shaped sauce boats of the middle period. About 1755.

56

A salt-glaze teapot of about 1750. The decoration is mostly blue and is painted directly on to the bright red ground.

Following Page

Above Left   A Liverpool pear-shaped teapot with palm column moulding and strawberry leaves on the base. About 1755.

Above Right   A Longton Hall teapot of about 1755 with birdshead spout. Painted mostly in puce.

Below   A unique pair of Bow monkeys. They are both dressed in yellow and puce, and lean against urns.

Left A Chelsea dish painted by O'Neale with Fable subjects. About 1755.

Above Two Nantgarn plates; on the left it was painted by Thomas Pardoe; on the right it is from the 'Duke of Cambridge Service' and has panels of flowers reserved on a turquoise or apple-green ground with 'pheasant-eyes' in gold.

A Derby biscuit group – 'Bacchantes adorning Pan' – modelled by Spengler about 1795.

One of a pair of seated griffins in Wedgwood Black Basalt. They support brass candleholders. They were made at Eturia about 1785.

Left   A Worcester dish painted with fruits and insects.

Below   Three Wedgwood dishes: *left* – Queen's Ware with a centre design of Coverham Abbey in Coverdale; *centre* – square compotier with a centre design of Stoke Guilford in Gloucestershire; *right* – Queen's Ware plate with a hand-painted border in brown and blue 'wheat' design, 1770.

Right A Spode plate with the 'Tumble-Down Dick' pattern.

Below Chelsea bird painting: *centre –* a circular bowl has two crested doves and two ptarmigan; *left and right* – a pair of tea-bowls and saucers en suite.

Above Left   A Liverpool bowl painted in colours with the frigate *Hyena* and a naval trophy. About 1780.

Above   A Wedgwood Creamware Jug with black-printed decoration.

Left   'Just Breeched' – the enamelled version by Chamberlains. About 1810.

Right A plate painted with birds in
a landscape by Dodson. About 1820.

Below A Milking Scene group
painted in over glaze enamels.
Probably by John Walton.
About 1820.

A Royal Worcester dish by Chamberlain about 1830. It has a view of the
Houses of Parliament and is surrounded by applied sea-shells and moss.
The whole is vividly enamelled.

4. Glass

Good-quality table glass has only been produced in England since the end of the fifteenth century. We may compare this with the industry in Egypt, which was established by 1370 B.C. or with that of Rome, which already held the secret of most of the methods of hand production and decoration that we know today. It is true that in the late Middle Ages window-glass and rough glass vessels were being produced, but the work was primarily in the hands of foreigners and cannot be compared with the glasses which the Venetians were producing at the same time. Yet, for two reasons, English glass occupies an important place in any history of glass production.

In the first place, it was in England that 'lead' glass was first produced successfully and on a large scale. This was the result of the work of George Ravenscroft (1618–1681) who, for the first time, obtained the silica needed for glassmaking from English instead of Venetian flints and added an oxide of lead called litharge. His glass was heavier than the Venetian glass, but superior in its brilliance and its remarkable light-dispensing quality. The simple and elegant designs of the end of the seventeenth century and the first half of the eighteenth century showed the glass off at its best, and the work of George Ravenscroft and the glassmakers who succeeded him not only produced the first authentic English style in glassware but also reached the high-water mark of English glass production for all time.

Collectors are no longer likely to come across glasses produced in England before Ravenscroft's time, and would probably not recognize them as such if they did, for they were produced by continental craftsmen in a style barely distinguishable from that of Venice or of l'Altare in Monferrat. Most of the examples that have been identified are in museums, and, if they came on to the market, would be extremely expensive. Few collectors go further back than the period of the baluster stem glasses (roughly 1675 to 1720). At first these had solid baluster or inverted baluster stems beneath a round funnel or V-shaped bowl, and were otherwise plain; but later the glassmakers began to embellish them with 'knops' of all shapes and sizes, drop knops, annulated knops, cushioned knops, acorn knops, egg knops, mushroom knops and many more. The bowls often had thick, solid bases, sometimes with a tear in them, and the usual shapes were the conical, the round funnel and the waisted.

Immediately after the accession of George I in 1714, a style appeared in England derived from the glasses of Hesse and west Germany, which we call Silesian. It featured a moulded pedestal stem which was ribbed and shouldered, four-sided at first but later, and more commonly, eight-sided. The style was also used for tapersticks, candlesticks and sweetmeat glasses.

By the 1720s the heavy baluster glasses in high quality metal were being replaced by a lighter style, for the manufacturers wished to make cheaper glasses that could be sold to a wider public. Thus began the period of the balustroid stem (1725–50). Glasses now had smaller bowls and longer stems. The 'Kitcat' glasses, named after a type which Kneller depicted the Kitcat Club using to drink a toast, were typical. They had a trumpet bowl on a baluster stem, with a plain section beneath and sometimes a base knop. The light baluster or Newcastle glasses (1735–65) were of a better quality than the balustroids, and, with their tall, slender, knopped stems, are some of the most elegant glasses produced. Newcastle was a very important glassmaking centre at this time, and its products were in heavy demand at home and also on the continent as they were better material for the engraver than the continental potash-lime glasses. The largest group of glasses made between 1740 and 1770 had plain straight stems, and were turned out cheaply and in large quantities. Some dram glasses have a heavy 'firing' foot: when club-members wished to applaud a toast or speech, they thumped the glass on the table and it made a noise like gunfire.

In the 1740s, what were advertised as 'wormed' or 'wrought' glasses began to appear. The glassmaker, by elongating and twisting a lump of glass containing air bubbles and forming it into a stem, created corkscrew and criss-cross patterns. Today we call them air-twist stem glasses. From 1750 onwards an even more startling result was produced by making similar criss-cross patterns with opaque white or coloured glass threads in the stem. The idea was by no means new, for it was related to the Roman *latticinio* style which the Venetians revived in the sixteenth century, but it was shown off to a peculiar advantage in the long, straight stems of the English glasses.

The last group of drinking glasses which can be categorized by the style of the stem alone is the group of faceted stem glasses. These were cut, usually with diamond- or hexagonal-shaped facets, which covered the stem, the foot, and often the base of the bowl. Most of them have round funnel, ovoid or ogee bowls, and many have a simple engraved pattern on the bowl.

Glasses might be decorated in one of three ways in the eighteenth century; by engraving, enamelling or cutting. Wheel-engraving first became popular in the 1740s with the appearance of the 'flowered' glasses. Scroll-work, flowers, vine-leaves and grapes were the usual motifs of a decorative border on a light baluster glass. But the English wheel-engraving was not of the highest standard, and consequently English glasses, especially Newcastle glasses, were sent abroad. Much of the work was done in the Netherlands.

Diamond-point engraving was also popular. It was used, for example, to record political events or to enable the wine-drinker to show his political allegiance – and perhaps tacitly to demand a similar allegiance from his guests. The most sought-after of these are the small group of Jacobite glasses known as 'Amen' glasses from the fact that they had some verses of the Jacobite hymn engraved on them ending with the word Amen. This is probably the only group of English glasses which has been extensively forged. They were made for a small number of important Jacobites. Most of these glasses belonged to Scottish families, and were engraved for them between about 1747 and 1750. There was a wide variety of less exclusive Jacobite glasses. Most of them, like the 'Amen' glasses, appeared after the Battle of Culloden Moor in 1746, probably over a period of about 20 years.

The Williamite glasses were also made in the mid-eighteenth century, probably on the fiftieth anniversary of the Battle of the Boyne, 1690, at which William III defeated James II. Generally, they bear an equestrian portrait, some references to the Boyne, and a quotation from the Orange Lodges' toast. On some of them the Irish harp appears. During the Seven Years War (1756–63) glasses were engraved with ships and portraits of Frederick the Great or Britannia and patriotic mottos. But it was not only the great events that were recorded on glass; many, for example, commemorate fierce local election campaigns.

The finest enamelling on glass is associated with William and Mary Beilby, who worked in Newcastle from about 1762 to 1778. They generally used a single colour, a bluish- or pinkish-white monochrome. With this they painted fine, delicate designs incorporating peacocks, ruins and obelisks, vines, rural scenes, flowers and fruit. William also did some armorial glasses.

Enamellers also worked on 'Bristol' glass. The name is used for an opaque white glass which has an appearance similar to porcelain. It was made in Bristol, but was certainly made elsewhere, too. The Newcastle glassmakers made Bristol glass, and it may well have been produced in the Midlands. The cream jugs, candlesticks, vases and tea-caddies made of 'Bristol' were often painted in oils or varnish and fired, and some were transfer printed. The standard of decoration varies considerably, for some pieces were bought from the factories and decorated by amateur home-craftsmen who sold them to the shops; while others were decorated by professional artists. Bunches of flowers, scrollwork, birds and *chinoiserie* were the favourite subjects.

Many people consider Bristol Blue to be one of the supreme achievements of the English glassmaker. As with 'Bristol' glass, the name is generic, not geographical. The glassmakers had to go to Bristol to obtain the colouring constituent 'smalt', which came to the Port of Bristol from Saxony, and so they called it Bristol Blue. The rich colour of this glass is shown off to its best advantage in the wineglasses and the decanters. Many of the latter had the names of drinks gilded on them; and sometimes a gilt label and chain round the neck of the bottle was simulated by means of gilding. Similar objects were also made in other colours, notably bright green.

Nailsea glass, on the other hand, was at first produced exclusively at Nailsea, near Bristol, though the style was later copied in other parts of the country. J. R. Lucas, who was a bottle-maker in Nailsea, decided to take advantage of the lower rate of tax imposed on bottle-glass by making domestic vessels out of it. Two kinds of decoration were developed: the *latticinio* or ribbon effect, which had already been revived for use in the enamel-twist glasses; and the colour-flecking used mainly on the dark Nailsea bottle-glass. The variety of the products of the industry are too numerous to list here, but the *latticinio* flasks are often seen, as are the rolling-pins, tobacco pipes and bells.

Cut glass has had a long and chequered career, Cutting was certainly used on some balustroid glasses. But in 1745/6 an excise duty was imposed on glass based on the weight of the materials, and manufacturers began to reduce the lead content of their glasses and use thinner metal which was not suited to the art of the cutter. Yet cut glass remained popular, though only on the stems of wineglasses could facet cutting still be used, for the bowls would only bear shallow fluting or stars. Then, from 1771 onwards, the excise duty was progressively increased. Ireland, on the other hand, had no such duty until 1825; and there was free trade between the two countries from 1780 onwards. It is no surprise, therefore, to find that many English glassmakers moved to Ireland, and established factories at Waterford and elsewhere. Cut glass returned to English factories when the excise was removed in 1845 in time to perfect, for the Great Exhibition of 1851, some of the ugliest glass that has ever been produced. But by then the American technique of press-moulding had made it possible to reproduce cut glass styles on a mould, and cut glass itself went out of fashion for a while.

There is no space here to deal with the multitude of ephemeral styles in glass that pleased the early Victorians. Few of them produced anything new. The fashion for coloured glass in the 1840s began in Bohemia in the 1820s. Apsley Pellatt's crystallo-ceramie process – by which cameo portraits were enclosed in cut glass objects or paperweights – was borrowed from the French. The

English *millefiori* paperweights were barely distinguishable from those the French had been producing before. This is not to say that all Victorian glass is worthless. The Northwood family, for example, perfected a cameo glass technique which enabled them to make passable imitations of even the Portland Vase. They also perfected the technique of etching on glass, so that the most fragile glasses could be decorated with etched patterns. John Northwood developed the 'intaglio' technique, producing a deeply engraved pattern with the kind of wheel usually used by the glass cutter. Engravers, too, had plenty of opportunity to show off their art on the globular decanters and heavy rummers of the period. About 1859 William Morris began the revival of good hand-made glass. Thanks to the work of such designers as Philip Webb and Christopher Dresser, and glassmakers such as those at Powell's Whitefriars Glassworks, quality glassmen began to concern themselves more with the design of their glasses than with their decoration, and this is the trend that has continued into the twentieth century.

The Buggins bowl – made by Ravenscroft in the late seventeenth century.
It has diamond point engraving.

An early and rare ale decanter in club
form with faceted-spire stopper.

A rare Anglo-Venetian goblet with trailed-line decoration and gadrooned lower cup on a spirally gadrooned stem.

A funnel-bowl goblet with gadrooned lower cup and baluster stem ornamented with raspberry punts.

A baluster goblet and cover.

A George II coin tankard with a scroll handle. The base contains a Maundy penny of 1744.

Left   A Beilby decorated ogee bowl wineglass with a gauze corkscrew-core stem.

Centre   An incised-twist wineglass with bell bowl and honeycomb moulding.

Right   A rare cylindrical stem glass with tears.

76

Left   Opaque twist ratatia glass: *centre left* – a Dutch–Newcastle wineglass with beaded and knopped-run baluster stem. The Arms are those of the House of Orange surrounded with those of the seven Provinces; *centre right* – an unusual cider flute with an appletree on the bowl.

Right   A baluster wineglass with ogee bowl.

Left   A flared bucket-bowl glass on a hollow square with Silesian stem.

Centre   An octagonal bowl wineglass with corkscrew and interlocking ribbon spirals stem.

Right   An ale glass with pan-top bowl.

Left   A Jacobean goblet bearing a portrait of the Young Pretender.

Right   A Jacobean wineglass bearing the rare motto 'REDI'.

A Williamite glass bearing portraits
of William and Mary.

A late Williamite decanter
commemorating the Battle of the
Boyne. About 1740.

Left   One of a pair of Irish lustre candlesticks with step-cut centres, button and finger drops. About 1815.

Below   A pair of vases and a pitcher jug with fine diamond cutting. Irish, about 1805.

81

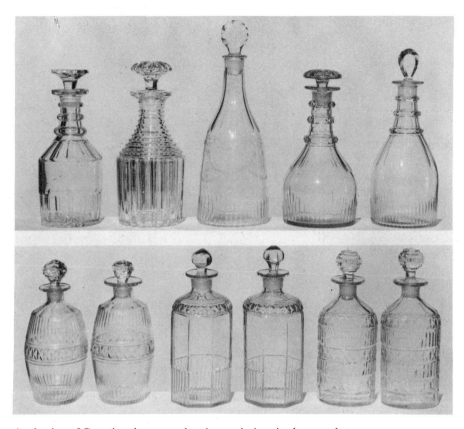

A selection of Georgian decanters showing variations in shape and stopper.
Dating from 1790–1820.

Left   An Irish Jeroboam decanter with mitre-shaped stopper. About 1790.

Right   A canoe-shaped cut glass bowl with star and lozenge cutting on a lemon-squeezer foot.

'a'   Bristol Blue condiment bottles with pear stoppers.
'b'   A set of Bristol Blue decanters with pear stoppers.
'c'   Bristol Blue condiment bottle. The labels are in gilt.

Opposite

Above   Two early Victorian perfume bottles: *left* – in gilded Bristol Blue glass; *right* – in Vaseline coloured cut glass.

Below   Bottles decorated with loops of coloured glass, one of the many varieties known as 'Nailsea'.

84

5. Clocks

It is reasonable to suppose that primitive man divided time into darkness and light. The year was an equally simple division based on such key events as seed planting, harvesting, migration of food animals and the like. The earliest method of telling time was by means of a sun-dial, the earliest recorded forms of which were used by the ancient Egyptians. They also used a 'clepsydra', a water-clock which measured time by the quantity of water discharged through a small opening in the body of the vessel. Also in use at about the same time was the sand-glass, the equivalent to our modern egg-timer.

Although there are no detailed written records of the first mechanical clock, it is safe to assume that it was well established before 1350; in fact, Giovanni di Dondi of Padua described a planetarium operated by clockwork which he made during the period 1346–1364.

So far as the actual timekeeping qualities of these clocks are concerned they were no real improvement; in fact, it was necessary to check daily against a sun-dial. At this period the clock was used to announce the times of masses. Clocks were, naturally, built for secular purposes and usually were housed in a town hall or specially built tower. Some of the clocks told more than the time. They indicated the position of the heavenly bodies and the important days in the Church calendar. The oldest known clock of this period in England is that at Salisbury Cathedral (c. 1386) which was reconstructed to very near its original form in 1956.

It is natural to expect that as soon as the tower or turret had been established there would rise a need for smaller versions. This in fact happened in the fifteenth century. It is interesting to note that up to this time clockmaking was an aspect of the blacksmith's craft, but with the need for much smaller components it became a craft for the locksmith.

The domestic clock was weight driven like its larger counterpart and showed no great difference in its mechanism. It was usual to add an extra wheel to each train to enable the clock to run with a proportionally shorter fall for the weight so that the clock could hang at a convenient height for its dial to be seen. In the case of turret clocks, the weights would run down a tower and it was not of great importance to limit their fall. Even so, the early domestic clocks would need winding every twelve to fifteen hours. The accuracy of the clock would have shown no improvement over that of its larger predecessor.

The weight driven chamber clock appeared about the end of the fourteenth century and was made with little modification until the mid-seventeenth. France, Germany and Italy produced the best known examples. Some of these early clocks were fitted with alarms and would be useful to arouse their owners from sleep. The clocks were not readily portable and would therefore have to be hung in the bedchamber, which limited their usefulness during the day. By this time the fashion of sleeping in a separate room would have become the accepted practice, and a portable time-keeper would have been extremely useful. The main difficulty was the weight drive.

The problem was solved by using a steel coiled spring as motive power instead of a weight. It was formerly believed that the spring came into use about 1500, but is now put as early as 1407. There were two main difficulties in the application of the main spring. The first was the making of the spring itself. In those days steel was only capable of being produced in small quantities and the quality could not be guaranteed. The second difficulty was that a spring exerts greater force when it is wound up than when it is nearly run down, and with the verge escapement this is fatal for accurate timekeeping. It was necessary, therefore, to provide some device to equalize the pull of the spring to get as nearly as possible a constant driving force. This was done by a means of a 'fusee'.

The spring driven clock was intended to stand on a table, and as it would be nearer to the person who wished to look at it it was possible to make the dial smaller than before. As time went on, smaller clocks began to be made, and by the early sixteenth century they were small enough to be carried on the person. In this way the watch came into being.

Table clocks could be divided broadly into two groups, those with vertical and those with horizontal dials. The horizontal dial group developed into the early watches. As the sixteenth century progressed, table clocks accrued astronomical and other subsidiary dials. France, Germany and Italy supplied the bulk of these clocks; Augsburg and Nuremberg becoming celebrated for their clocks. The table clock marked a definite break with tradition in that the mechanism became boxed in; i.e. the clock had a case. The early wall clocks consisted simply of the mechanism with a little decoration, and the movement of the wheels could be seen.

There were no native craftsmen capable of making a clock until the late sixteenth century. Edward III granted a charter of protection to three 'Orologiers' in 1368, one of them coming from Delft, and they were allowed to exercise their craft in the realm. They probably worked on clocks for the King at Westminster, Queensborough and Langley about this period, and the clocks at Salisbury and Wells have also been attributed to them.

Repairers of clocks were known in Britain from the Middle Ages. For instance there is a reference to 'Roger the Clockmaker' being sent from Barnstaple when Exeter Cathedral clock needed repair in 1424, and the 'clokkemaker of Kolcester' (Colchester), repaired a clock for the Duke of Norfolk in 1483. The word 'make' was at that time synonomous with 'mend', so it cannot be assumed that these 'clockmakers' actually made clocks or did anything else than repair or maintain existing clocks. Henry VIII possessed a number of clocks and watches, all of which must have been imported from the Continent or made by visiting workmen. Elizabeth I also owned many clocks and watches and had her own clockmaker in the person of Nicholas Urseau who was of French descent, but her clock keeper was Bartholomew Newsam who received the office of clockmaker in 1590 on the death of Urseau, and thus became the first English Royal Clockmaker.

Mention should also be made of Randolph Bull who made the

clockwork for Thomas Dallam's organ which was presented by Queen Elizabeth I to the Sultan of Turkey in 1599. Bull later became Royal Clockmaker.

The style that emerged in Elizabeth I's reign and ended about George III's is probably known as the 'Lantern' clock, but is also known as 'Cromwellian' or 'Bedpost' and by various other names. Late examples in which the dial is much wider than the movement are called 'Sheepshead'. The movement of these clocks was basically the weight driven wall clock of the Continent, but most of the metal used was brass and the clock was generally not placed so high. A wheel balance was always used. So far no evidence has been forthcoming of an English Lantern clock with a foliot. The design would not allow for this, as the bell was not very far from the top plate of the movement, and was flanked on three sides by frets which would have rendered the adjustment of the small weights difficult. Regulation of a Lantern clock would always have been carried out by increasing or decreasing the amount of lead shot carried in a hollow on top of the going weight, and thereby altering the amount of driving force available.

The Lantern clock at first had a narrow chapter ring with stumpy figures. The hour hand was of sturdy construction to permit of its being set to time, and the inner edge of the chapter ring was engraved with quarter marks to allow the time to be read with greater accuracy. As the seventeenth century progressed the dials became larger and the figures longer, and after the invention of the pendulum, minute hands were added. Smaller versions with an alarm only and no striking work were produced for travelling purposes. The popularity of the style lasted until long after they had ceased to be made as a regular item of the clock-maker's output. During the nineteenth century many old clocks had their movements replaced by contemporary spring driven ones and were adapted for standing on a mantelpiece, which is quite out of keeping with this type. Later still, small versions with platform escapements were sold for use on desks or bedside tables.

To offset foreign monopoly the King was petitioned to establish a guild for the regulation of the clockmaker's craft in London. In 1631 the Clockmakers' Company controlled the training of the future members of the craft, carefully limiting their numbers so that the market should not be flooded with clocks.

By the middle of the seventeenth century clockmaking had reached a comparatively high standard. Table clocks were being made with various astronomical indicators, and their movements included parts made of brass. The weight driven wall clock became refined into the Lantern clock in England and in other countries it was subjected to improvements and new forms of decoration. The only disadvantage was that all instruments of this period were shocking timekeepers. Errors of a quarter of an hour to an hour a day could be expected, and a clock that gained one day might lose the next. Great efforts were made to correct this, the most successful device being the pendulum.

Although Galileo (1564–1642) wrote on the pendulum, the name that will always be associated with the use of the pendulum to control a clock is that of Christiaan Huygens (1629–95). The Dutch physicist made his experimental model on Christmas Day 1656 and obtained a patent in 1657. He commissioned a clockmaker in The Hague, Saloman Coster, to produce the clocks, and Coster turned out some excellent work incorporating the new principle.

The early pendulum clocks broke completely new ground in clock design. These clocks were so far ahead of their time that until recently many people regarded them as Victorian. Most noticeable was the use of a wooden case, which was almost unknown at the time, while internally there was the pendulum itself and also the use of a direct drive from the mainspring without the use of a fusee. The movement was virtually that of a table clock turned on its side, while the pendulum was very short, as the verge escapement was retained, involving the pendulum swinging through a wide arc. It was now at long last worthwhile to fit a hand indicating minutes.

As soon as the invention of the pendulum became known in England, John Fromanteel, a member of a family of clockmakers of Dutch descent living in London, went to work for Coster to learn how the new type of clock was made. An invention that brought the accuracy of a clock to within a few minutes per day was something that would be eagerly sought after by every clockmaker.

The introduction of the pendulum into clockwork marked the beginning of the period of almost two centuries during which the London makers led the world into craftsmanship and invention.

Not until the mid-nineteenth century, when the London makers refused to move with the times, was that supremacy lost. The restoration of the monarchy in 1660 meant the end of the period of austerity enforced by the Commonwealth, and the people were ready to spend money to refurnish their homes in the latest style. We find at this period that architectural designs in ebony were the fashion for clock cases, and British makers quickly abandoned two of the main features of the Dutch clocks. They connected the pendulum directly to the verge, doing away with the separate suspension and the cheeks in one blow, and they also did away with the velvet ground to the dial, preferring matted brass or later plain brass engraved and spandrels made of cast brass applied separately.

Development in the late seventeenth century was rapid. The severely architectural styles of the sixties evolved into the basket top of the 1680s. Ebony remained a favourite wood for cases, but clocks tended to get taller as the century progressed, and movements became technically more refined. No record of this period would be complete without mentioning the name of Thomas Tompion. He acquired the title of 'The Father of English Watch-making', and was buried in Westminster Abbey. Six thousand watches and five hundred and fifty clocks have been listed, which means that he could not have made them all with his own hands. Such production could not have been achieved without a large staff of skilled workmen, and it is perhaps as the first 'production engineer' rather than as an horologist that Tompion ought to be remembered.

The usual name for spring driven pendulum clocks of the seventeenth and eighteenth centuries was 'Bracket Clocks'. These clocks were not usually placed on brackets, which implies a permanent home, but were rather intended to be carried from room to room and were even provided with a carrying handle for this purpose. Many of these clocks had no striking mechanism but were provided with a cord which could be pulled to make the clock repeat hours and quarters; a very useful feature when the clock stood on a bedside table during the night.

The introduction of the pendulum not only led to a development of the spring clock as first created by Coster, but also produced an entirely new design of clock. The old clocks with foliot or wheel balance would have needed winding every twelve to fifteen hours and at the same time it would be necessary to regulate them every day after comparison with a sundial. Most public clocks had a sundial nearby for this purpose. After the clock had been made so accurate that the daily regulation was no longer necessary, there was an incentive to prolong the intervals between winding. Spring driven pendulum clocks in their early days were made to run for one day, then two or more and finally eight days between windings. During the early years of the reign of Charles II, London makers evolved a new type of clock which would run for eight days. The movement was generally similar to that of the spring clock except that the drive was by weights supported by catgut lines which were wound round brass barrels, and the clock was wound by means of a key through the dial as were the spring clocks. The short pendulum was retained as the verge was still the only available escapement. The ebony architectural case was provided but the clock was intended to be hung on the wall. The Dutch spring clocks were usually hung on the wall but also had feet for standing on a table. Spring clocks in England were seldom seen with this feature. The exposed weights of the new type of clock were provided with polished brass containers, but even so they were considered unsightly and clocks were produced with a long tall cupboard below them to hide the weights from view. The next step was to make the cupboard and the top into a free standing unit and the 'Long-Case' clock was born. (It is more popularly known as the 'Grandfather Clock'.)

The earliest were quite small, being only about five feet high, and the ebony architectural style was used for the cases. The Fromanteel family was associated with this type in the early days. The movements were closely allied to the pendulum controlled spring clocks which were being produced and which were direct descendants of the Table Clocks. The Long-Case clock is therefore more closely connected with the Table Clock than with the weight driven wall clock.

The advantages of a longer pendulum were being considered at this period as it would be more capable of receiving fine adjustments in length and therefore the regulation of the clock would be more exact. By having fewer beats per hour fewer teeth would be necessary in the wheels, thereby saving labour.

There has been a lot of discussion on the subject of whether Robert Hooke or William Clement, a London clockmaker, was the inventor of the anchor escapement. A very strong point in Clement's favour is that he was originally an anchor smith, and the shape of the anchors on which he worked no doubt suggested the escapement. He also made clocks with a pendulum five feet long beating a second and a quarter. These early clocks had cases very little larger than the short pendulum type, but as the century progressed there was a tendency for the Long-Case clock to get bigger, especially when examples were produced which ran for one, three or six months between windings. The earliest clocks with a very long period of running were three made by Tompion in 1676 for Greenwich Observatory. These clocks were intended to be wound only once a year.

The Long-Case clock rapidly became popular after the invention of the anchor escapement. The cases at first had an ebony finish and later marquetry and parquetry became popular, while in the eighteenth century lacquered cases were fashionable. In the early part of the same century walnut also occurs, and once mahogany had established itself its popularity lasted until the end of the English Long-Case clock in the nineteenth century.

The Lantern clock was still being made in the eighteenth century, but many movements of the Lantern type were also being produced with square brass dials intended to be covered by a hood and hung on the wall, or else to be fitted in a country version of the Long-Case. One encounters many of these one-handed clocks in a variety of cases not always pleasing to the eye, and in many cases a minute hand has been added. This can always be detected when the old dial is retained, for the original dial has quarter hour marks inside the hour figures and no minute marks outside them. Some of these clocks have movements with the wheels held between two brass plates as on the eight-day clocks, but they are still to be considered as belonging to the Lantern family. In their final form down to about 1850 they were produced in Birmingham with the usual painted iron dials found on nineteenth century clocks. By this time most of the eight-day movements and dials were being produced there, with the name of the vendor painted on the dial to order, and the cases would be made to the order of the purchaser in his own locality.

As the Long-Case clock increased in size, the dial tended to increase also. Beginning with a size of about nine inches square immediately after the Restoration, dials had increased to twelve inches square by about 1690, and early in the eighteenth century an arch was placed above the square dial. Early arches were made separately, but soon the dial and arch were being made in one piece. One of the earliest arch dials is to be found on the Tompion clock in the Pump Room at Bath. Dials at this period were made of sheet brass with silvered chapter rings and cast spandrels fitted separately, but as the eighteenth century progressed some dials were made with the figures engraved directly on to the dial itself, or else the dial was silvered all over and the figures were indicated in black. This led the way to the painted iron dials characteristic of the late eighteenth and early nineteenth centuries.

As soon as the arch was added to the dial it became a space that needed filling. Sometimes a plaque with the maker's name and place of business was put there, or a strike/silent hand would occupy that position. After about 1730 the phases of the moon were indicated by a disc bearing two moons that rotated once in two lunations, and this neatly filled the space in the arch. The square dial was mostly used on the thirty-hour Lantern type movements, but had a longer life on eight-day clocks in Lancashire and Wales where it would sometimes include moon phases in an opening below the figure XII. Moon dials often include an indicator to show high tide at a certain port, but this has to be specially calibrated for the place in question and is of no use elsewhere. The day of the month was indicated at first by a figure showing through a square opening above figure VI. Later a dial was placed here or a kidney shaped slot allowed figures on a disc to be visible. The seconds hand placed below figure XII goes back to the early days of the anchor escapement, for with a pendulum beating seconds and a scape-wheel of thirty teeth the division of the minute can be indicated on the dial with very little extra trouble. The eight-day clock is recognizable at a glance by the winding holes in the dial, but even this can prove a trap for the unwary. Less fortunate people who could not afford an eight-day clock would sometimes have false winding holes painted on the dial of their clock to give the impression that it was an eight-day one when in fact it was only a thirty-hour clock and would be wound by pulling the chain or rope inside the trunk.

The Long-Case clock became particularly associated with England. The only other country that took it seriously was Holland, and tradition was still strong enough to keep it popular in the U.S.A. after 1776, although native American styles drove it off the market there before it had disappeared in England. In the latter country, its popularity in London waned during the later part of the eighteenth century, but it was still popular in the provinces, particularly in the north, and the mill owners made rich by the Industrial Revolution always desired very flamboyant styles for their homes, helping to create distinctive types for Lancashire and Yorkshire as the eighteenth century gave way to the nineteenth. The type was also popular in Wales and Scotland.

Front view of a Lantern clock by
William Bowyer. About 1635.

Rear view showing the construction and
arrangement of the mechanism.

A Great Chamber clock by William Bowyer. About 1630.

The movement of a Long-Case clock by Jas. Clowes. About 1685.

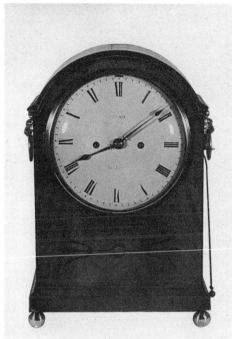

A bracket clock with a cord to make it repeat the hour.

A Gothic clock by James Garland. About 1820.

Opposite Above

Left   A very early spring driven pendulum clock.

Right   A small lantern-type clock. About 1720.

Below

Left   A bracket clock with strike and day of month by James Markwick. About 1670.

Right   A bracket clock with handle for carrying from room to room.

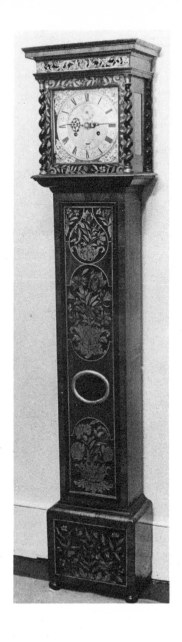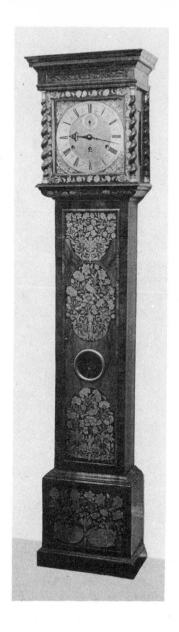

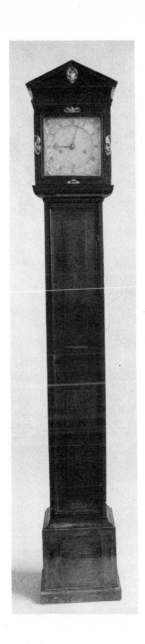

Left A Regency Long-Case clock.

Opposite
Left A month Long-Case clock by David Guepin. About 1690.

Right A quarter chiming Long-Case clock by Henry Jones. About 1690.

6. Pewter

Pewter is an alloy whose essential ingredient is tin. It was made by the Romans, some of it perhaps in England, for the raw materials of the trade – tin and lead – were readily available. In the early Middle Ages, pewter was regarded as a respectable alternative to the rarer metals. An ecclesiastical synod of Rouen in 1074 permitted chalices to be made of pewter in default of gold and silver. By the thirteenth century though, the chalices that were now used at Mass had to be gold and silver, whereas pewter chalices were made to be buried with the priest. By the end of the Middle Ages, however, the market for pewter was expanding rapidly. Men were breaking out of the strict gradations of the social structure that was based on the landlord-tenant relationship, and the 'new-rich' – the yeoman, farmer and urban shopkeeper – were willing to spend money on household utensils worthy of their status. At the same time, new techniques were being mastered in England. The seventeenth century saw the first indigenous production of table-glass in England, and pottery was becoming an industry. By the next century glass was being made for ordinary people and so was china. Now it was pewter that became vulgar though it was not finally ousted until the Victorians learnt that it was not respectable not to have silver in one's canteen and under one's candles, and china and cut glass on one's table.

The composition of pewter became standardized at an early date. During the reign of Edward III the London pewterers petitioned the Mayor and Aldermen of the City of London for legislation designed to protect their trade from 'unfair competition' (i.e. to make a closed shop of the trade), and to assure the good quality of English pewter. The result of their persuasions was the Ordinances of the Pewterers of 1348. It was provided, among other things, that all flat-ware (plates and dishes) were to be of 'fine pewter, that is with the proportion of copper to the tin, as much as of its own nature will take'. All other objects wrought in pewter by the trade (for instance, cruets and candlesticks) were to have a composition of 26 pounds of lead to each hundredweight of tin; a very similar substance later became known as 'lazy' metal. Though not mentioned in the Ordinances, an even poorer quality of metal was generally used where loss of shape was not important and a fine appearance was not needed, as in the case of commercial objects and toys. In 1473, the industry was well established, for in that year it was granted its first charter and took its place among the City Livery Companies.

A further enactment of 1503 also helped to maintain standards. This made it compulsory for makers to put their marks, known as 'touches', on their products. It became the custom – no one knows exactly when – for the maker to stamp the impression of his mark on a panel of metal, a 'touch plate', which was kept in the Pewterers Hall. There is a complete record, therefore, of all London pewter makers going right back to those who began work in the 1640s.

Pewter marks were primarily used to identify the maker. They were not intended, like silver marks, to date the piece. The date of a piece of pewter can only be guessed at by examining the style and discovering the dates of the maker.

Marks were also used to register good or bad quality. In 1474, base pewter was disfigured with a 'broad arrowhead', later to be forfeited and destroyed. A good quality piece of pewter might be officially stamped, in 1509, with the 'lily pot' and the 'strake', both of which appear in the Companies' arms, or with the fleur-de-lys in 1548. The rose and crown was variously used, sometimes as a mark of quality, often without official approval, sometimes to show that the goods were intended to be exported. The crowned letter 'X' had a very chequered career, although it was originally used to denote hard metal.

In addition to the maker's touch and the marks mentioned

above there are often four small marks, very like silver hallmarks in appearance, on pewter. These usually contain the initials or the name of the maker. If they contain a date, it will be the date of registration of the touch, not the date of manufacture. In some cases they contain the initials of more than one maker, and it has been suggested that this signifies some kind of trade arrangement between makers, by which one maker preferred to specialize or because they'lacked the ability or the equipment to make certain pieces.

A great deal of pewter is not decorated at all. It is a material eminently suited to show off the virtues of fine, simple designs and throughout most of its career it was modelled in pleasing, functional shapes. Yet there was also some fine decorative work done in pewter, especially in the seventeenth century.

A style of decoration was dictated to a large extent by the nature of the metal. It was too soft to be line-engraved really successfully, and a completed engraving was easily worn smooth. In any case, the closed shop prevented not only manufacture, but also decoration, of pewter by outsiders so that artists were excluded from the work. Yet there are good examples extant of one kind of engraving, known as 'wriggled-work'. For this, the engraver used a gouge-like tool with a sharp, narrow blade, which he held at an angle and pushed across the metal, rocking the blade from side to side all the time.

A rarer kind of decoration was achieved by means of a punch cut with an ornamental design in relief which was transferred to the pewter, like the touches, by resting it on the pewter and giving the reverse end a blow from a hammer. Continuous ornament could thus be built up around the border of a plate, composed of crescents, roses, fleur-de-lys or other conventional designs.

The commonest method of decorating hollow-ware was to make a pattern on the inside of the mould used to cast the piece. The object would thus be made and given cast decoration in a single process.

The range of pewter produced was very great and it is difficult to categorize it satisfactorily. The division into flat-ware and hollow-ware covers many of the better-known kinds of pewter – plates, chargers and porringers coming under the former and drinking vessels, measures, candlesticks and cruets under the latter – but this does leave out things like spoons. However, this simple division, with the addition of one or two extra-curricular items, is probably the best for a short general survey.

Flat ware, also commonly known as 'sad-ware', was beaten by the maker to ensure maximum strength, and this rule, together with the regulations about composition, were strictly enforced by the Pewterers' Company. Fine pewter had always to be used for the group of closely related items that commonly appeared on the table – plates, dishes, chargers, platters and trenchers. Dating these pieces is difficult, especially if they were made before the seventeenth century. In the early seventeenth century pewterers were making broad-rimmed dishes with no decoration on the rim, and they continued to do so until the third quarter of the century, though the width of the rim gradually decreased. From about 1675 the rim began to be decorated, at first with multiple reeding gouged out on a lathe, later with reeding cast on to the surface as part of the process of making the dish. Cast moulding continued to be standard during the first half of the eighteenth century, though the reeding was usually single. In the last period of pewter manufacture the reeding disappeared altogether, though the moulding on the underside of the plate rim was thickened.

The Ordinances included porringers among those vessels which were required to be made of 'fine' metal. These were small, shallow vessels, with a flat, horizontal handle or handles, and they were used for liquid or semi-liquid foods. In the mid-sixteenth century they were made with two ears cast in the form of a fleur-de-lys, while from the beginning of the seventeenth century onwards it was established practice to have one ear only. The early blood porringers or bleeding bowls are probably not distinguishable from their contemporary porringers, indeed the two may have been to a large extent interchangeable. Some bleeding bowls, however, have lines inside to mark liquid capacity. Smaller bowls, on the same pattern as these, are probably wine-tasters.

Larger, two-handled cups have to be classified according to the purpose for which they were made, and this is not always clear. There are the 'caudle cups', used to give spiced wine drinks, usually for a medicinal purpose, and the posset pots, which cannot be clearly distinguished from each other, though posset – a drink with a base of ale or sack combined with cream, sugar and nutmeg – is quite different from caudle. Toasting cups were larger again, as they were made to be handed round the table and supply the whole company with drink. The wassail bowl was generally used for mixing the drinks at table. Both are related to the smaller loving cup, which, at least in its later days, was intended to be a memento, and was engraved for presentation at weddings. Incidentally, few footed loving cups were made before the middle of the eighteenth century.

A great deal of church pewter has survived from all periods, for, though it had been rendered obsolete by silver, it was carefully preserved in the churches until recent times when the new fashion for collecting pewter made it financially worthwhile to sell it all off. In particular, this meant that many of the fine pewter flagons have been preserved in excellent condition. The typical flagon made before 1675 had a body of a tapering cylindrical form, a plain curved handle and a moulded foot, which grew wider as the century progressed, and a bun-shaped cover or in the case of the 'Beefeater' flagons, a lid shaped like the caps of the Yeoman Warders of the Tower. From the end of the seventeenth century the most common type was of a tall cylindrical shape topped with a domed cover surmounted with a finial. In defiance of the London fashions, some acorn-shaped flagons were produced in Yorkshire and are thus called 'York' flagons.

Pewter plates with flat rims and deep central wells, which many churches possessed until the early twentieth century, may have been proper patens – plates intended to hold the bread at communion – but were probably used latterly as flagon stands, if they had not been originally made for that purpose. Alms dishes, too, were made of pewter and a few of them were elaborately decorated.

The drinking vessels and measures are probably the best known pieces of pewter. Pewter drinking vessels have probably been made since the industry began, though early examples cannot be accurately dated. We know that 'tanggard potts' and 'stope potts' were being made in the fifteenth century, and many varieties of beakers, bowls and cups in the sixteenth century. The Stuart beakers were tall and slender enough to be elegant, but in the eighteenth century beakers tended to become squat and stumpy.

The early tankards were probably not distinguishable from measures, but flat-topped tankards were being made in the last half of the seventeenth century. Domed covers appeared shortly before 1685, together with a new type of handle terminated by a 'ball' or, from 1710, by a 'fish-tail'. From 1730 onwards the tulip-shaped tankard became more typical, normally with a domed cover. Tapering, lidless tankards were also produced in consider-able quantity in the eighteenth century.

The earliest identifiable measures are the baluster measures, which probably originated in the mid-sixteenth century, though measures had certainly been made in pewter long before that. But pewter may never have had the field to itself, for throughout the seventeenth century the pewterers complained about and peti-tioned against the use of earthenware measures. The baluster shape continued to be standard throughout the history of pewter, though some variety was achieved on lidded measures by varying the design of the thumb-piece. The bulbous spirit measures known as West Country or 'Bristol' measures are of a quite different, jug-like shape.

Pewter candlesticks were probably made from the earliest period until metal was ousted by brass and silver in the eighteenth century. The 'bell-based' style candlesticks were probably being made at the beginning of the seventeenth century. Octagonal bases largely disappeared during the reign of Queen Anne, when the drip-tray also became obsolete, giving way to the plain baluster form.

Everyone knows that peculiar significance was attached to salt until recent days and some sufficiently grand Master Salts were made, together with the smaller varieties which became popular from the seventeenth century onwards.

From the fourteenth century to the mid-seventeenth century, spoons had bowls that were broader at the base than they were next to the stem, that is the reverse of the present day spoon bowl. A spoon was often made distinctive by the knop which terminated the usually six-sided stem. It is the tremendous variety of these knops that attracts the collector: the 'ball' knops of the late four-teenth century; the 'horned-headdress' knop of the fifteenth century; and the 'alderman', 'strawberry' and 'apostle' knops are among the many attractive types that may be discovered.

Two late-Victorian sugar-sifters.

Top Three fine early candlesticks, the centre specimen being slightly later than the others. Note the large drip-trays.

Above A rare eighteenth century water canteen. Could possibly be earlier.

Top A set of seven Irish haystack measures running from a gallon to a half-noggin. Made by Austen & Son in the early nineteenth century.

Above Three tankards showing various types of handle. They run from quarter-pint to pint.

Top Left   A late-seventeenth or early-eighteenth century jug holding a quart with right-angled handle.

Top Right   A Regency baluster tankard holding a pint.

Above   A pair of small candlesticks dating from the late eighteenth century.

Top Left A rare Victorian finger-bowl. Note the interestingly decorated rim.

Top Right A late-eighteenth century snuff box with chased decoration all over. It is about 3 inches long.

Above Left Tankard with lid and Maltese Cross thumb-piece.

Above Right A Victorian coffee pot with high domed lid, falcon finial and ornate engraving and decoration.

Top   Late-Victorian tea-set of teapot, milk-jug and sugar-bowl.

Above Left   A biscuit-barrel with lion's-head masks holding ring handles.
About 1900.

Above Right   A mid-Victorian fruit-bowl with hammered decoration.

113

7. Victoriana

Until quite recently most people could not hear the word 'Victoriana' without a look of distaste crossing their faces. We became accustomed for a time to being told that men always looked down on the work of their fathers, found the work of their grandfathers quaint, but never spared themselves in their admiration for their great-grandfathers. It was to be merely a matter of time before we all sighed with pleasure at the sight of a Victorian armchair or a piece of press-moulded glass, and sentimental china figures and Valentines would soon have us clapping our hands with delight. To a certain extent this has happened. People now spend a great deal of money on collecting Victoriana, but they are different people from those who still follow the tastes of the eighteenth century. The two ages are as far apart in their attitudes to domestic decoration as they have ever been, and it will probably always be so, for the machine age destroyed all continuity in the spheres that it was able to affect. One can only appreciate Victoriana, then, by taking a quite different attitude to it. And that attitude involves thinking of each object as a manifestation of the period that produced it, not evaluating it according to how it has managed to combine functionalism and beauty. Those who find little to appreciate in the life-cycle of the average Victorian are bound to remain cold to the charms of Victorian period flavour.

We are not talking here of the fine arts during the Victorian period, nor of those restless spirits who found the Victorian way of life quite as repulsive as its detractors of today and who worked towards a new order, in the arts as well as in society in general. It would be wrong to put the Victoriana label on the work of the Pre-Raphaelites, who had this, if nothing else, in common with other artistic movements, that they were trying to do something new. Wrong, too, to put such a label on the work of the great Victorian designers – William Morris, C. R. Mackintosh, Christopher Dresser – who, more or less, escaped from their own age.

We may set the tone by starting with the Valentine. In the eighteenth century this had been a hand-written affair, decorated by the hand of the suitor, but the Victorians took advantage not only of etching and lithography, but also of all kinds of outlandish techniques and materials for decorating these mass-produced cards – simulated flowers, paper-lace and ribbons, paper cut in Gothic patterns and coloured gold or silver, shells and feathers. A favourite topic was a card of a church door or window – extravagantly Gothic, of course, which opened to reveal a marriage ceremony in progress, and was captioned with some commonplace verses:

> *May thy bosom thus incline –*
> *To a faithful heart like mine,*
> *Ever loving – ever true –*
> *A counterpart – my love of you.*

Another one was the 'marriage nest', depicted as just that: a rustic thatched cottage perched in a bird's nest, surrounded by flowers and foliage. Others took themselves less seriously, and went so far as to send humorous Valentines: Valentines in the form of banknotes for example, drawn on the 'Lover's Banking Company', and promising to pay on demand the entire love of 'the suppliant who sends this'.

The Valentine eventually had to give way in the face of the Christmas card however; a much more commercial venture, for though a few reckless gentlemen might send more than one Valentine, everybody could send large numbers of Christmas cards. In fact, social pressures made it compulsory for them to do so. The early Christmas cards – they were becoming really popular by the 1870s – followed the designs of the Valentines with plenty of paper-lace and tinsel. Later, Christmas gathered around it its own motifs: robins, berries, holly, snow, bonneted ladies stepping from coaches into the snow to greet their friends on the festive day. Some of the better known Victorian designers applied themselves to Christmas cards. Walter Crane produced some delightful, flowing Art Nouveau designs, and Kate Greenaway made cards and calendars with precocious little girls in long frocks and beribboned hats dancing round the borders.

For period flavour, there is nothing to beat the Victorian photograph. The daguerrotype process was becoming known at the very beginning of Victoria's reign, and at the same time W. H. Fox Talbot was conducting the experiments that led him to the production of the calotype, the first of the negative-positive pro-cesses. But, throughout the period, photography remained a very complicated business requiring a very great deal of cumbersome equipment, and a considerable amount of patience in the sitters, who had to pose for long periods before the camera without moving. It is partly this that gives Victorian photographs their characteristic appearance: the look of frozen immobility in the faces and the staring eyes.

We may take, for a moment, a diversion into the nursery and look at the juvenile drama, a curious development of the tinsel pictures of popular actors that were sold in the early part of the nineteenth century for the delight of adults. Sheets of paper were sold, either 'penny plain or twopence coloured', on which were depicted the actors and scenes from some choice stage production of the time. These could be cut out – and, if necessary, coloured – and mounted on cardboard. The scenes are done with all the exaggeration of a pantomime set, while the figures take up the most extraordinary stiff poses, usually with the right leg straight out and left knee slightly bent. Character is revealed by means of the clothes and by highly formalized hand and arm gestures, the faces usually being completely expressionless. Also in the nursery are some much sought-after toys. The better doll's houses are probably the best record we have of the appearance of a room in an ordinary Victorian house, for the wallpaper, curtains and upholstery fabrics, chair, table and bed designs are all authentic and down to scale, even including pictures on the walls,

116

decorative pottery and cooking pots. The life outside is also recorded in the most remarkable detail – carts, carriages, trains and animals. The sophisticated child might have a clockwork automaton combined with a musical box – though it would probably have been made in Germany – or a pair of clowns who could be made to tumble slowly down stairs over each other's backs by the ingenious contrivance of joining them with mercury-filled rods.

The fittings of the Victorian house – notably the oil lamps – have now become fashionable, so much so that it even seems to be worth the trouble of reproducing them. As Victorian houses are modernized it may be possible to obtain some of the more permanent fittings, such as toilets, which were profusely covered with Gothic decoration, or other fashionable motifs. The bathroom began its career late in Victorian days, and it seems unlikely that many genuine Victorian bathrooms remain, but one can still find the movable fittings, such as the ewer and basin, and the chamber pot. All kinds of external decorations for the house can be obtained from demolition contractors, and this was a field in which the Victorians achieved some good effects. There are cast-iron balconies and pleasant cast-iron street lamp brackets for suspending above doorways. A great improvement can be made in the fireplaces of Victorian houses if the correct cast-iron grate and decorative surround is installed.

Reverting to period flavour, we would do well to mention the Victorian poster. The posters for Victorian melodramas speak eloquently – as the plays themselves did, in a rather crude form – of Victorian attitudes, especially moral attitudes. The stock-in-trade of these melodramas – the unfaithful wives, the evicting landlords, the distraught heroine, and the hero who mistakenly believes himself to have been guilty of some hideous crime – varied but a little, like the characters in a pantomime, requiring only a little rearrangement. The posters were not always pictorial; sometimes they are purely typographical, the title and the main characters being in huge, black letters, sometimes aligned rather drunkenly on the page. But the designers of pictorial posters had a rich field of choice in their search for macabre illustrations. Oddly enough, in view of this, their products are frequently lifeless, like the characters in the juvenile drama; the actors are shown in entirely conventional poses, with the hero or the detective stretching out his arm in accusation, and the villain shrinking back, non-plussed. Towards the end of the century, however, the role of the poster altered completely, and it then became an acceptable art form. In France, this change will always be associated with the names of Toulouse-Lautrec, Cheret and Mucha, but the same wind of change was blowing in England too, where D'Oyly Carte, the head of the opera company that performed the works of Gilbert and Sullivan, decided to encourage better poster design in England by attaching an artist to his Savoy Theatre as their regular poster designer. The artist he chose was the talented Dudley Hardy, whose work showed the strong influence of Art Nouveau ideas in design, especially in his use of large areas of flat pattern, and tortuous, flowing lines. This kind of work, as well as the strikingly memorable designs of Aubrey Beardsley, affected not only the design of theatre posters, but all kinds of advertisements.

Victorian illustrated books and magazines had a character all of their own and are an excellent field for those who find them attractive, for there is still so much available. The standard vehicle for the illustrator from the late 1850s almost until the end of the century was the wood and steel engraving, and this medium was used in such a spate of fine illustrations in the 1860s that 'the illustrators of the Sixties' has become an acceptable chapter heading for a remarkable period of art history. Some of the illustrations to the greater Victorian novels have never been properly superseded, so that George Cruikshank's illustrations for *Oliver Twist* are still familiar to children today, and have become an almost essential part of the book. Phiz (whose real name was Hablot K. Brown) did some equally memorable illustrations to Dickens, as well as others for the less known novels of Lever and Ainsworth. Our impressions of Alice and the White Rabbit are still formed from the drawings of Sir John Tenniel, engraved by the eminent Brothers Dalziel; and Kate Greenaway's books of poems and drawings of children continue to be printed without a change. Indeed, the Victorian children's book was very highly regarded by artists, and gave rise to Randolph Caldecott's Picture Books, and attracted Walter Crane, who later made such an impact in the field of design, especially Art Nouveau design. Crane shared many things in common with William Morris, who probably produced the finest of all Victorian books at his Kelmscott Press.

But we are straying from what is strikingly Victorian. Far more so among books, are those filled with the luminous colour illustrations of Miles Birket Foster, perhaps the 'prettiest' of Victorian painters. We may also mention some of the cartoonists of the Victorian period. We have already referred to John Tenniel as a book illustrator, but he was also the chief cartoonist of *Punch* for a long time. George du Maurier quietly satirized the life and fashions of the Victorian middle classes in such a way that they themselves could smile at them, while Charles Keen drew some rather more hot-blooded cartoons of life among the ordinary people of his generation. Phil May, who drew for *Punch* towards the end of the century characterized the same kind of people but in a simpler and very pleasing style, obtaining strong effect from a few well-chosen lines.

Here we have only been concerned with the 'miscellanea' of the Victorian Age. More important things like furniture, silver, etc. are dealt with in the individual chapters devoted to these subjects.

Left A cane basket of cotton flowers under a protective glass dome; a typical example of Victoriana.

Right Glass oil-lamp decorated with a traditional snow scene.

Opposite

Above A stone cameo brooch and two shell cameo bracelets set in pinchbeck (an imitation of gold). These date from 1850 to 1860.

Right Mourning jewellery in 'French Jet', the name used for black glass used to imitate jet.

Far Right Maughan's patent gas geyser, made in 1868.

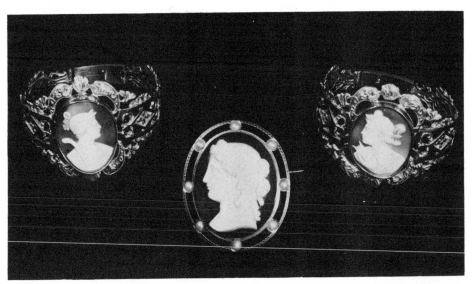

FOUR PATTERNS FOR NETTED ANTI-MACASSARS DARNED IN WOOL.

THE ANTI-MACASSAR COMPLETE.

EXPRESSLY DESIGNED FOR THE ENGLISHWOMAN'S DOMESTIC MAGAZINE.

Opposite
Doll's House of about 1865. These toys are very good guides to design trends, as they were furnished down to the last detail in the latest fashion.

Above Designs for antimaccasars from *The Englishwoman's Domestic Magazine.*

Left Wax doll with carved wooden body and sleeping eyes. About 1850.

123

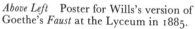

Above Left   Poster for Wills's version of Goethe's *Faust* at the Lyceum in 1885.

Above Right   A very popular Valentine theme. The doors of this embossed and gilded card open to reveal a marriage ceremony.

Right   One of Sir John Tenniel's illustrations for *Alice in Wonderland*.

Opposite

Top   Calendar for 1884 by Kate Greenaway.

Below   An anecdotal fan painted in the Kate Greenaway style, about 1880.

124

An early photograph of William Ewart Gladstone with his grandson. It was taken in 1875.

Index